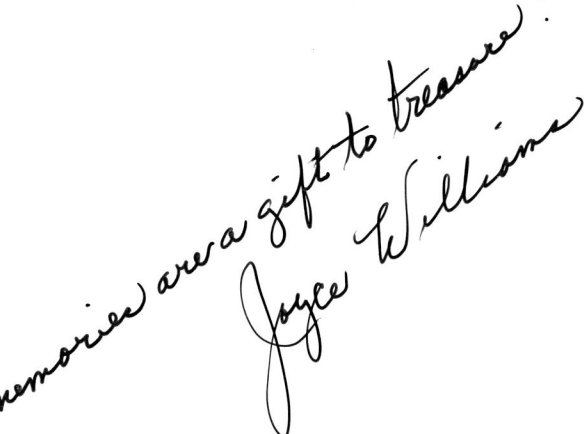

MW01612078

Robbie Remembers

written by Joyce Williams
illustrated by Betty Radwin

For permissions or additional copies, contact:

Missions, Ministry and Media Foundation
13432 Blanco Road #188,
San Antonio, Texas 78216
Phone: 210-846-4192
Email: jwilliams56@satx.rr.com

First Edition
Design: Teri Nave

Library of Congress Cataloging-in-Publication Data
Williams, Joyce 1926-
Robbie Remembers / Joyce Williams
ISBN 0-9762549-0-5
1. Children and death. 2. Grief in children. 3. Children-memories.
4. Children-Counseling of.
I. Title

The knot in Robbie's stomach tightened.

The pain increased with each step.

1

Grammy and Robbie made their way to the back of the small white church.

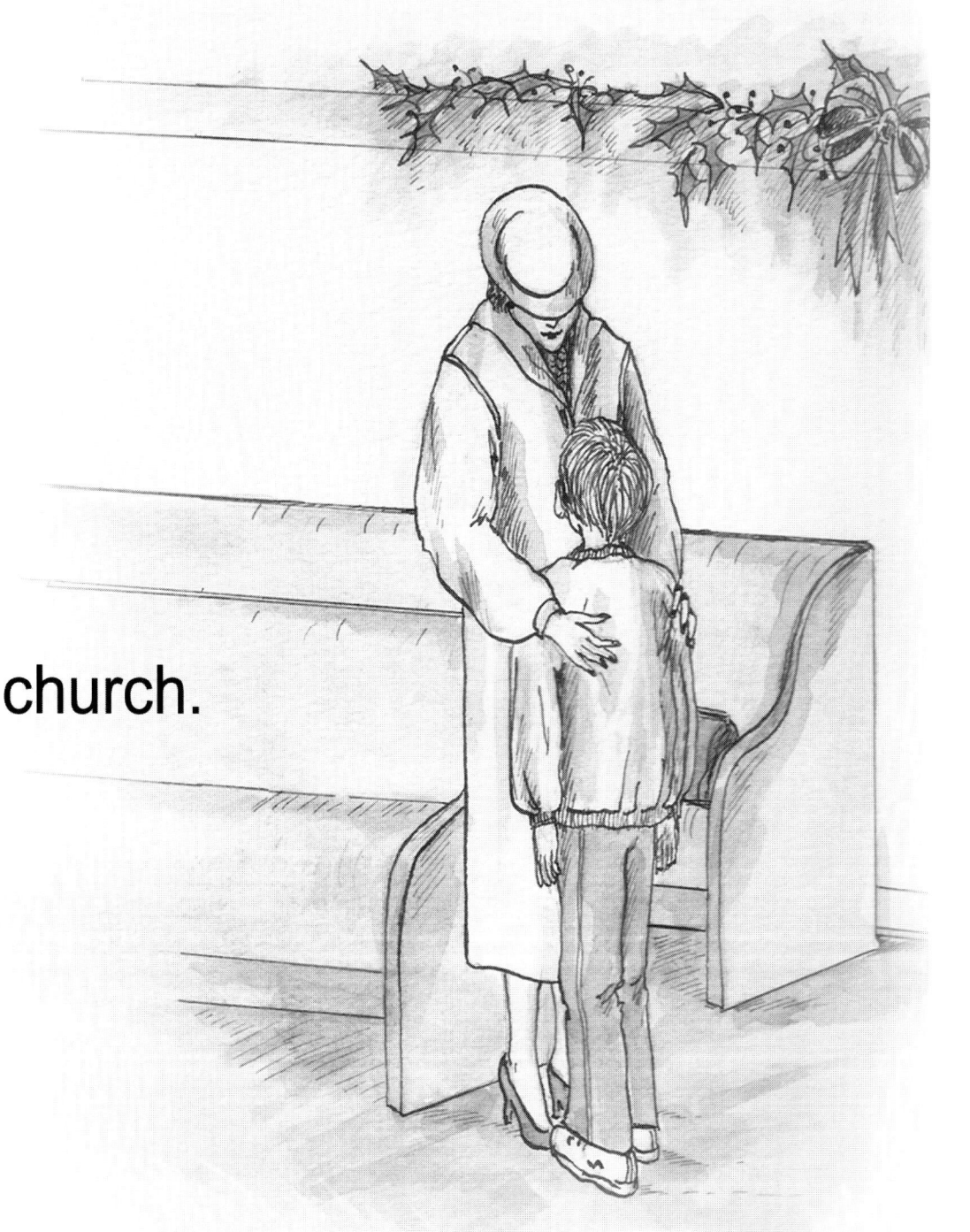

So, why did Robbie
have trouble breathing?

Why did his stomach
feel like it was
tied in knots?

Robbie remembered

coming to this church

when he was small.

He sat on the back pew

and entertained himself

until the service was over.

But never on Christmas Eve.

Tonight candles, greenery and poinsettias
decorated the altar.

Smells of Christmas filled the air.

The choir, in their silver robes,

looked like angels.

They moved quietly into the choir loft.

Robbie was restless.

Maybe he needed to go
to the bathroom.

Why did he feel so yuk?

Was he going to be sick
to his stomach?

The service was beginning.

Without warning,
tears began to form.

Would they spill over
on his new clothes?

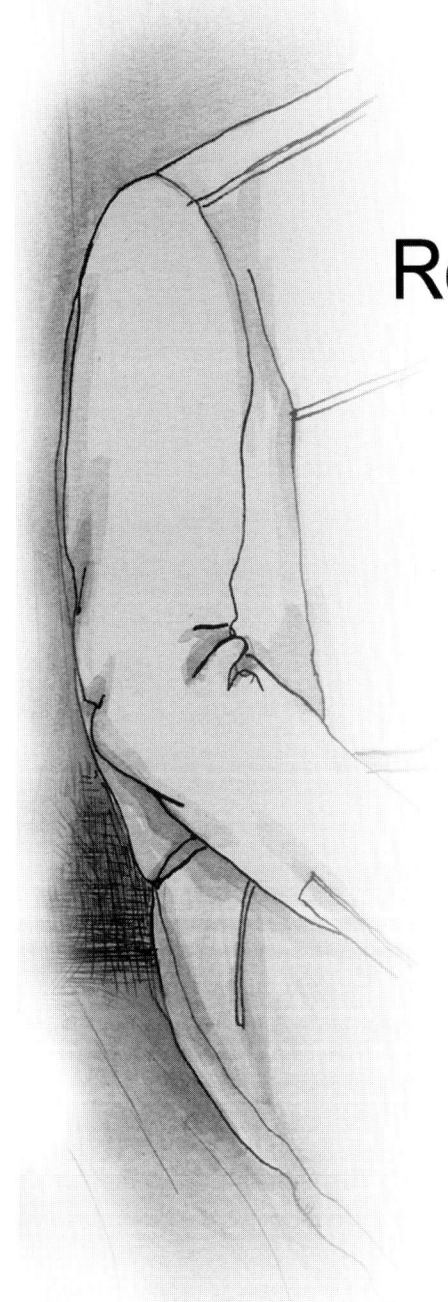

Robbie tried not

to think about times

Daddy Luke had sat

on this same pew.

Robbie dug his fists
into his pockets.

He studied the toes
of his shoes.

Why did he miss Daddy Luke so much?

Why hadn't he stayed home?

At last the hymn was finished
and everyone sat down.

When the minister said,
"let us pray."

Robbie was glad
to close his eyes.

Grammy's purse was on the seat
between them.

She slipped her hand inside

and handed Robbie a tissue.

Then she found some cards

and a pen.

Robbie fought against

the terrible feeling inside.

He coughed,

sneaked a look

at the people

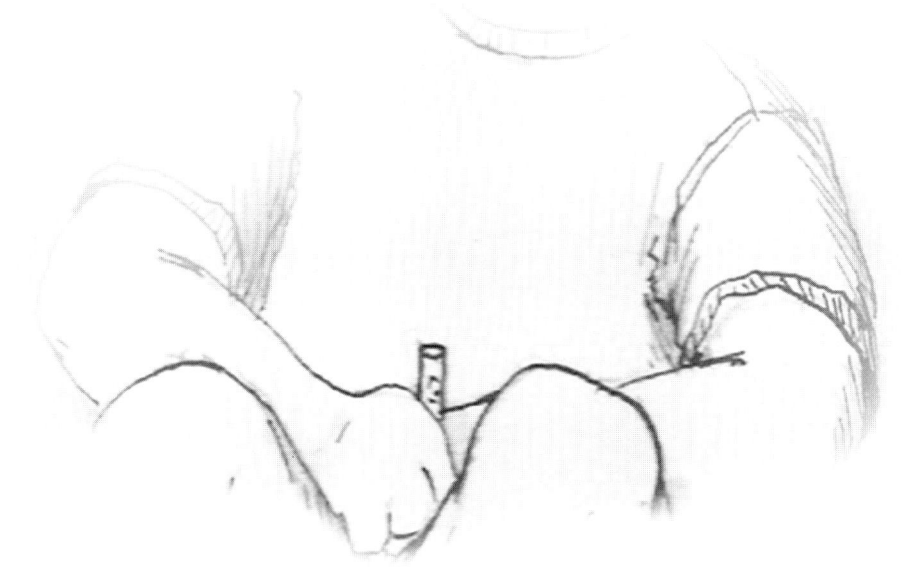

beside him,

and hurriedly began to draw.

Robbie remembered

rides in the old pickup truck.

and talks with Daddy Luke
in the tree house.

Tears spilled over.

Grammy whispered,

"It's all right, I miss him too.

Let's go home, Robbie."

To Parents

ROBBIE REMEMBERS is a tribute to a loving grandfather. When an important person, like a grandfather dies, children need an opportunity to cry, express their feelings, and share with a trusted adult. Reading this book with a child can provide a time to remember. Not all experiences may be pleasant, but ask a simple question, "How was it different with your grandfather?"

Death brings fears. When a death occurs, because their understanding of death is limited, children need answers. Two worrisome questions children may never verbalize are "Did I do something that made this person die?" Or, "Will I die, too?"

When children sense something is wrong but no one explains, their fears and fantasies may become giants. Tell children the truth - in simple terms.

If children have good memories, as Robbie did, build on them, review them and celebrate them. If memories are lacking, search for ways to create new ones. On a grandfather's birthday, a child may release a balloon for each decade of his grandfather's life. Or plant a tree and measure its height. The following year, check the tree's growth.

A child old enough to love is a child old enough to treasure memories.

Betty Radwin

Encouraged by her daughter, Sarah, Betty Radwin, who lives in Boerne, Texas, has illustrated her first children's book, *Robbie Remembers*.

A retired teacher, Betty has discovered her love for sketching southwest Texas landscape and rediscovered her love of seeing the world through children's eyes.

The pen and ink illustrations show a sensitivity which enahnces the text and gives freedom to the imagination of young children.

Joyce Smith Williams

Joyce Williams, a certified bereavement facilitator, lives in San Antonio, Texas. A retired Montessori teacher and school administrator, Joyce is a widow who enjoys cooking, organic gardening, classical music, church activities, spending time with her five grandchildren and traveling.

Joyce began writing in high school. She wrote curriculum for Sunday School teachers for ten years. Additionally, she published two children's books in the 70's. She resumed writing after retirement 1993.

Later she served as a pediatric chaplain for six years at Methodist Children's Hospital and for the last eight years as a program coordinator for the Children's Bereavement Center of South Texas. Recently *Triumph Over Grief*, her memoir, was published in Austin, Texas.

Lord, teach me to smile again,
But never let me forget I cried.

Other publications by Joyce Smith Williams...

Chronicling a twenty-year period, *Triumph Over Grief*, is the very personal story of how Joyce Williams coped with the deaths of her husband, daughter, two grandsons and the murder of a very dear friend. The story speaks to those who wrestle with loss, those who recognize the fragility of life, and those who move on in spite of grief.

(Available through the Missions, Ministry and Media Foundation.)

"I received your book, opened it and sat right down and read it from cover to cover. I was moved by your honesty and vulnerability."

"I sat down to read and never got up from my chair until I read it through."

"A powerful, moving story which is a tribute to God's strength."

Children's Books

Available through Children's Bereavement Center of South Texas (www.cbcst.org)

> *I Remember Mama*
> *I Miss My Little Brother*

No longer in print

> *Adjustable Julie*   *Sue is New*
> *Pedro's Pinata*   *Gus is Grouchy*
> *Sam is Mad*   *Fred Needs Friends*

Articles and Stories

"Sarah's Memory Box" - published in Aries 2000 - Texas Wesleyan University's journal of creative expression
The Fog Lifts, A Perfect Healing, and Cadence of My Heart - all three articles published in
> The Journal of Pastoral Care and Counseling
"Old Rattler and the King Snake" - published in Boys' Quest Magazine

Questions to discuss after reading
Robbie Remembers

1. What three things did Robbie see in the little white church?

2. What did Robbie wear on Christmas Eve?

3. What made Robbie's stomach hurt?

4. Who was the special person Robbie remembered?

5. How did Robbie try to hide his feelings?

6. Who else was feeling sad?

7. What did Grammy bring in her purse?

8. Would you give this story a different name?